I Wonder Why

Whales and Dolphins

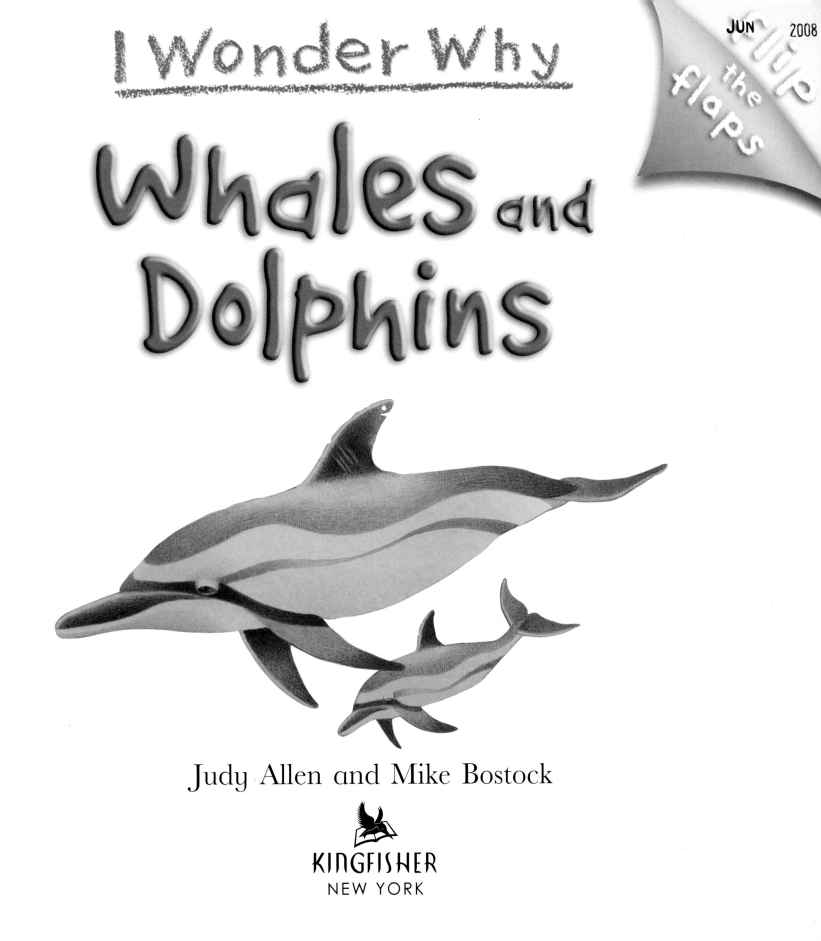

Judy Allen and Mike Bostock

KINGFISHER

NEW YORK

Copyright © 2008 by Kingfisher Publications Plc
KINGFISHER
Kingfisher is an imprint of Macmillan Children's Books, London.
Published in the United States by Kingfisher U.S., a division of
Holtzbrinck Publishing Holdings, Limited Partnership,
175 Fifth Avenue, New York, New York 10010.

Distributed in Canada by H. B. Fenn and Company Ltd.

Library of Congress Cataloging-in-Publication Data
Allen, Judy.
  I wonder why flip the flaps whales and dolphins / Judy Allen.—1st ed.
      p. cm.
  Includes index.
1. Whales—Juvenile literature. 2. Dolphins—Miscellanea—Juvenile literature. I. Title.
  QL737.C4A44 2008
  599.5—dc22   2007030938

ISBN: 978-0-7534-6225-6

Consultant: Stephen Savage

Kingfisher books are available for special promotions and premiums.
For details contact: Director of Special Markets, Holtzbrinck Publishers.

First Hardback American Edition April 2008
Printed in China

10 9 8 7 6 5 4 3 2 1

1TR/1207/LFG/UNTD/140MA/C

1. Where do whales
and dolphins live?

2. Do they get cold
in the water?

3. Are whales and
dolphins fish?

sperm whale
flicks its tail
out of the water

1. Some live in icy oceans, some live in warm oceans, and there are dolphins who live in rivers.

2. Whales and dolphins have a thick layer of fat under their skin, called blubber. This keeps them warm.

3. No. Fish have blood that is as cold as the sea and breathe in air from the water. Fish and dolphins also swim in different ways.

How fish and dolphins swim

tail fins move from side to side

parrotfish

bottle-nosed dolphin

tail fins move up and down

5

Breathing

Whales and dolphins have to swim to the surface in order to breathe air. They breathe through blowholes on the top of their head. Some whales dive down very deep and have to rise up a long way to breathe in air.

The blue whale is the biggest whale.

6

1. How long can whales hold their breath when they're underwater?

2. Does water go into their blowholes when whales and dolphins dive?

3. Can you see them breathing?

blue whale
breathing out

1. How do the babies learn to swim?

2. How big are baby whales and dolphins?

3. Do their mothers feed them?

1. They can swim as soon as they are born, although they may be a little unsteady at first.

2. Quite large—usually the mother is only three times as big as her calf, and the calves grow fast.

3. At first they live on their mother's milk. She will teach them to eat what she eats when they are older.

pilot whale calves feeding

newborn pilot whale drinking its mother's milk

young pilot whale chasing a squid to eat

9

Food

Most whales and dolphins eat fish. Some dolphins hunt fish in groups. They swim around the fish to make them move close together so that they are easier to catch. Baleen whales eat tiny creatures called plankton.

orca, or killer whale, catching a seal

dolphins hunting fish

10

1. What is a killer whale, or orca?

2. Do dolphins spit out the fish bones?

3. How do baleen whales catch tiny plankton?

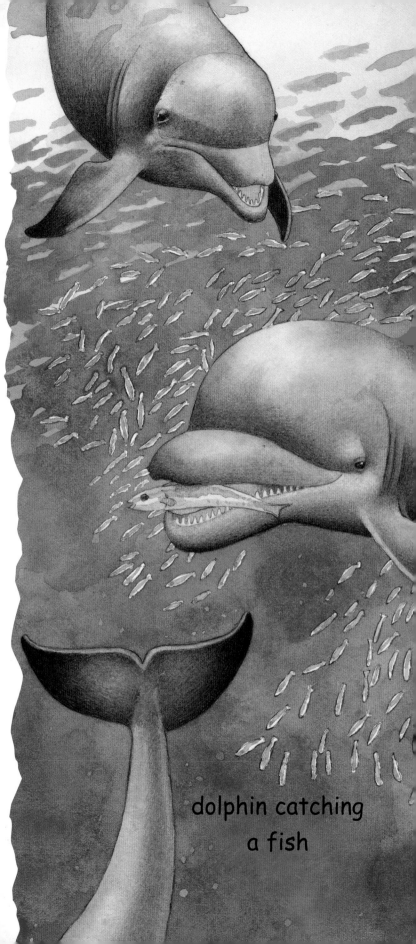

dolphin catching
a fish

1. Killer whales, or orcas, are the largest dolphins. They eat fish, birds, and even seals.

2. No. They swallow the fish whole. Dolphins cannot chew.

3. They suck in water that is full of plankton—then push out all the water and swallow the plankton.

southern right whale feeding (a type of baleen whale)

sucking in water that is full of plankton

baleen

water is pushed out through the baleen and then the whale eats

11

bottle-nosed dolphins
squeaking

bottle-nosed
dolphins

1. Baby dolphins learn to talk by copying their mothers.

2. Humpback whales sing when they want to attract a mate.

3. Some scientists think that beluga whales may talk by making faces.

Beluga whales

They live in Arctic waters.

They are also called white whales.

They eat fish, squids, and crabs.

Traveling

Some whales make long journeys called migrations. The greatest traveler is the humpback whale. Groups of humpback whales spend the summer in icy oceans and then swim to warm water in the winter.

humpback whales
in icy waters

14

1. There is more food to eat in icy oceans, but they like to breed and have their babies in warmer waters.

2. No one knows why they don't get lost. The oceans are their world, and they understand them.

3. We can see them from boats and sometimes from the shore. We also track dolphins from the patterns on their fins.

watching dolphins from a boat

fin

Each dolphin has a different pattern on its fin.

15

Do whales and dolphins play?

There is still a lot that we don't know about whales and dolphins, but we are certain that they play. Whales breach, and spinner dolphins leap out of the water and spin and somersault. Bow riding and wake riding look fun too.

common dolphins
wake riding

16

1. How do whales breach?

2. Do spinner dolphins really spin?

3. What are bow riding and wake riding?

humpback whale breaching

common dolphins bow riding

1. Whales jump right out of the water and then fall back in with a huge splash.

2. The spinner dolphin can leap up in the air and turn seven times before it falls back into the ocean.

3. Bow riding is being carried along by the front wave of a moving boat. Wake riding is traveling in the wave behind a boat.

spinner dolphin spinning

17

Index